D1222691

THE SCARIEST PLACES ON EARTH

STANLEY HOTEL

BY DENNY VON FINN

BELLWETHER MEDIA · MINNEAPOLIS, MN

Are you ready to take it to the extreme?
Torque books thrust you into the action-packed world
of sports, vehicles, mystery, and adventure. These
books may include dirt, smoke, fire, and chilling tales.
WARNING : read at your own risk.

Library of Congress Cataloging-in-Publication Data

Von Finn, Denny.
  Stanley Hotel / by Denny Von Finn.
    pages cm. -- (Torque: the scariest places on earth)
  Includes bibliographical references and index.
  Summary: "Engaging images accompany information about the Stanley Hotel. The combination of high-
interest subject matter and light text is intended for students in grades 3 through 7"--Provided by publisher.
  ISBN 978-1-60014-950-4 (hardcover : alk. paper)
  1. Stanley Hotel (Estes Park, Colo.)--Miscellanea--Juvenile literature. 2. Haunted hotels--Colorado--Estes
Park--Juvenile literature. 3. Ghosts--Colorado--Estes Park--Juvenile literature. I. Title.
  BF1474.5.V66 2014
  133.1'2978868--dc23
                                                              2013008245

TABLE OF CONTENTS

CHAPTER 1

NO SLEEP AT THE STANLEY HOTEL

You have had a great day exploring the beautiful Rocky Mountains. Now it is time for some sleep. You climb into your soft hotel bed and shut off the lamp. You start to doze off. Then a sound jolts you awake.

Are those footsteps outside your door? Who could be coming for you this late?

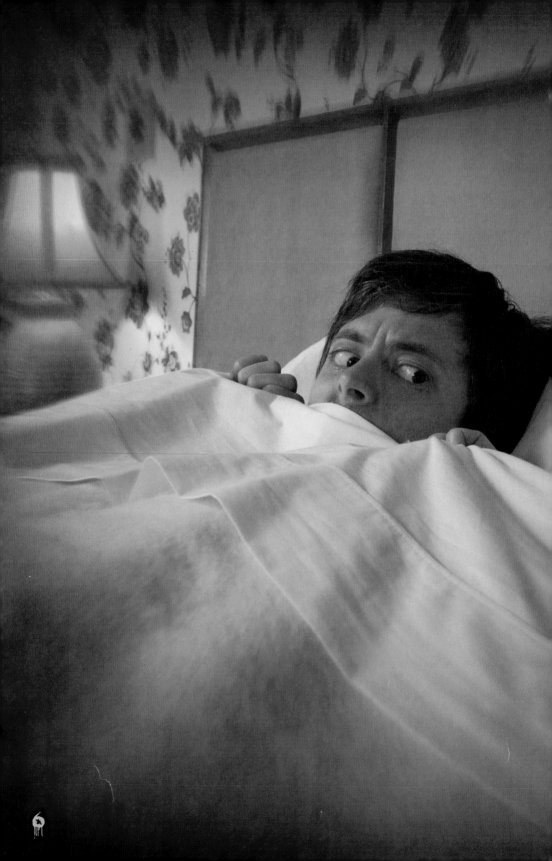

You pull the blanket to your chin. You cannot remember if you locked the door. Did the handle just rattle? You catch a flash of light out of the corner of your eye. It will be a long, sleepless night at the Stanley Hotel!

CHAPTER 2

THE HISTORY OF THE STANLEY HOTEL

The Stanley Hotel of Estes Park, Colorado is one of America's most haunted places. It was built by a wealthy businessman named F.O. Stanley. Stanley and his wife, Flora, moved to Colorado in 1903. The fresh mountain air was good for Stanley's poor health.

F.O. Stanley

The Stanley Hotel opened in 1909. A number of bad accidents took place in the hotel's early years. One worker was buried alive in a tunnel beneath the hotel. In 1911, an explosion blasted housekeeper Elizabeth Wilson through the floor of Room 217. She was badly injured, but she lived.

The Stanley's most famous event happened in 1974. Author Stephen King and his wife stayed there just before the hotel closed for the winter. They were the only guests.

The couple stayed in Room 217. That evening, King had a nightmare. In it, his young son was running through the hotel halls and screaming. The **eerie** dream led him to write the horror story *The Shining*.

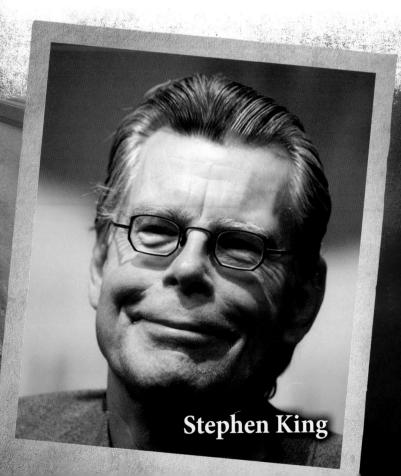

Stephen King

CHAPTER 3

A NIGHT AT THE STANLEY HOTEL

In 1980, a movie based on *The Shining* made the Stanley Hotel even more famous. Today, thousands of visitors stay there each year. They say that the spirits of the Stanley Hotel often greet them after the sun goes down.

JUST DROPPING BY

Hotel workers say that Flora Stanley's ghost likes to play the piano in the ballroom. Others have seen F.O. Stanley behind the front desk.

A scene from *The Shining*

15

Child ghosts are among the Stanley's most common spirits. One couple left after complaining about loud children playing in the hallway. But there were no children staying at the Stanley that night.

EVP recordings have captured voice-like sounds throughout the hotel. One child has been heard calling for his nanny.

Paranormal activity has been reported in most of the hotel's 140 rooms. Visitors in Room 217 have heard footsteps near their bed in the dead of night. Some have seen lights turn on and off. Others have returned to the room to find their bags packed. Perhaps Ms. Wilson wants the room to herself.

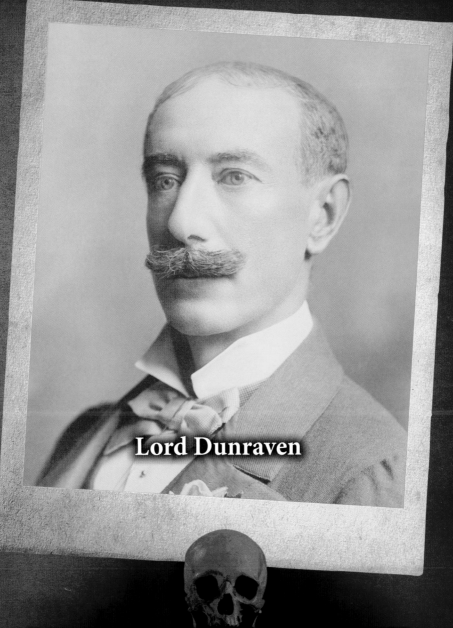

Lord Dunraven

THE GHOST OF LORD DUNRAVEN

F.O. Stanley bought the land in Estes Park from a man named Lord Dunraven. Lord Dunraven was an unpopular man in the area. He was known for trying to steal land. His ghost has been seen in Room 407. It is even believed to have stolen guests' jewelry!

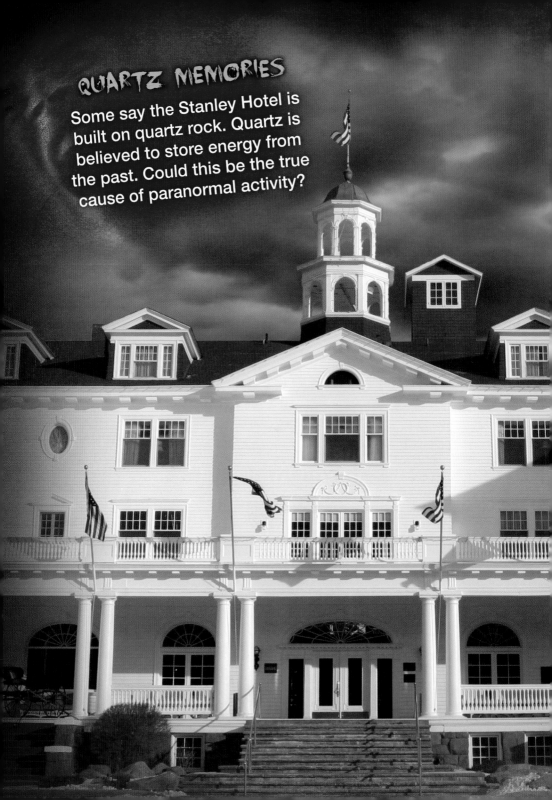

QUARTZ MEMORIES

Some say the Stanley Hotel is built on quartz rock. Quartz is believed to store energy from the past. Could this be the true cause of paranormal activity?

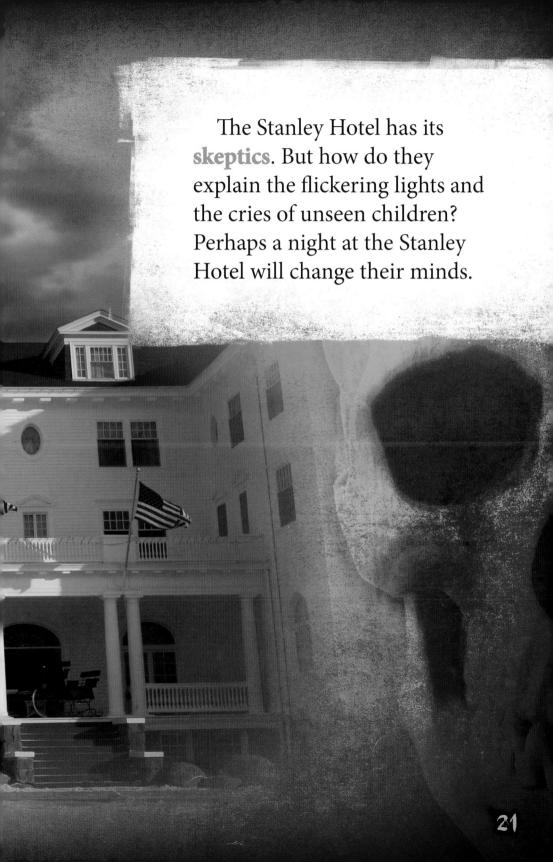

The Stanley Hotel has its **skeptics**. But how do they explain the flickering lights and the cries of unseen children? Perhaps a night at the Stanley Hotel will change their minds.

GLOSSARY

eerie—strange and scary

EVP—electronic voice phenomena; EVP recordings sound like speech but have no known source.

paranormal activity—strange events with no known explanation

skeptics—people who do not believe in something

TO LEARN MORE

AT THE LIBRARY

Gee, Joshua. *Encyclopedia Horrifica*. New York, N.Y.: Scholastic Inc., 2007.

Parvis, Sarah E. *Haunted Hotels*. New York, N.Y.: Bearport Pub., 2008.

Whiting, Jim. *Scary Places*. Mankato, Minn.: Capstone Press, 2010.

ON THE WEB

Learning more about the Stanley Hotel is as easy as 1, 2, 3.

1. Go to www.factsurfer.com.

2. Enter "Stanley Hotel" into the search box.

3. Click the "Surf" button and you will see a list of related Web sites.

With factsurfer.com, finding more information is just a click away.

INDEX

The images in this book are reproduced through the courtesy of: Robert Kelsey, front cover (top), pp. 2-3 (background), 20-21; Darla Hallmark, front cover (bottom), pp. 16-17; Croisy, front cover & p. 21 (skull); James Frank Stock Connection Worldwide/ Newscom, pp. 4-5 (left); Stephen Coburn, p. 5 (right); Williams + Hirakawa/ Getty Images, pp. 6-7 (left); Robert Naratham, p. 7 (right); Corbis, p. 8; "Danita Delimont Photography"/ Newscom, p. 9; Christopher Badzioch, p. 10; COSfoto, p. 11 (woman); Ian Cumming/ Getty Images, p. 11 (fire); Peter Talke Photography/ Pete Talke, p. 12; Varley/ SIPA/ Newscom, p. 13; Warner Brothers/ Album/ Newscom, pp. 14-15; Juan Vte. Muñoz, p. 18 (background); Lario Tus, p. 18 (ghost); Bettmann/ Corbis, p. 19.